A jacklillyandfriends publication

Original Watercolours © Holly Leavett-Brown

© Gerald Smythe 2014

Designed and produced by Omicron Reprographics

www.omicronrepro.co.uk

Lilly and Six

'I'm certain Lilly is putting on weight. She does not seem to be herself at the moment. I'm sure she's getting fatter. She keeps making a bed in the wardrobe too', said Jack to himself.

'But she doesn't even sleep in there!
Hmmmm it's all very strange. Perhaps she's eating my food.
I'll keep an eye on her.'

The next day, Lilly went to the vets.
The first thing she did when she returned home was to finish the biscuits in Jack's bowl.

Jack and Lilly both love long walks in the country. Running through the woods is their favourite thing to do. Playing under the trees and through the bushes, excited by the many wonderful smells and sights to see.

Oh *Lilly!*

Lilly loves to swim in the little pool at the bottom of the woods.

'Come on Jack!' squeaked Lilly excitedly.

'We're off for a walk YIPEEEE!! Quick, quick let's go!'

'Alright, alright! I want to come too, but I'm not swimming. I've told you enough times, Lilly!'

Lilly didn't run as fast as she usually did, but she still dived into the cold pool and swam around.

Lilly and Jack both had a lovely time, as they always did, running on forever and ever, until it was time to go home.

Each day, Lilly's tummy was growing
bigger and bigger and Jack was concerned
for his friend.

'Are you OK, Lilly? You don't seem yourself lately. You don't run as fast as usual
and your tummy is nearly as big as mine! I am worried for you, and despite our
differences, I hope you know that I love you very much.'

'I am fine, thank you, Jack. I think we may have some visitors arriving soon. Let's see how you much you love me then, ay!'

'Visitors! Coming to see us?! When?'

'Of course not! Don't be silly, Jack!'

'Oh. *Silly Lilly!*'

As the weeks went by, Lilly had grown to be a round little dog with a big, BIG tummy!

Hmmm! What could possibly be happening to little and large Lilly?

One very cold morning in December, just before Christmas, Lilly made herself very comfortable in her special new bed under the prickly branches of the Christmas tree.

Except Lilly was not going to sleep.
She was hot, panting, and very restless.

'Jack - Jack!
Hey, Jack, where are you?
Please come here, Jack! I've got something to show you!'

'I'm on my way, Lilly! I thought you were asleep!'

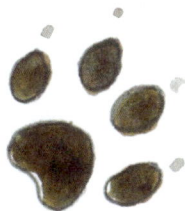

Jack entered the lounge to find Lilly and six tiny puppies underneath the Christmas tree. 'Oh, Jack – look! Meet my little puppies! Gosh, I'm so tired. Do come and see them!'

'Good gracious! Did Father Christmas bring them down the chimney? Just where did they all come from? I must have dozed off! It's not Christmas Day, is it?'

'Come closer, Jack! Take a look at my gorgeous puppies!
Slowly and quietly. Be careful not to scare them, Jack!
They are so precious.'

'Wow! They are so tiny! Oh, they are so beautiful and cute!
Hmmmm. I still don't understand!'

'These are my puppies, Jack! That explains why I have been eating lots and lots recently. My tummy has had six puppies growing inside it. I've been busy burying food all over the place, too! I have to make sure I have food stored up and hidden safely.'

'Jack, did you know, it takes nine weeks for puppies to grow inside a tummy? That's why I haven't been so quick on my feet lately. Having six puppies inside me has been tiring and I'm exhausted. I am so pleased that they are all healthy. And now I have six little wet noses to look after!'

'Six puppies! My goodness! Are they all staying here? Where are they all going to sleep?'

'No, Jack. In a few weeks after Christmas when I stop feeding them special milk, they will all go off to new homes, with new owners to love and care for them.

I have names for them all, too! Noel, Cracker, Humbug, Sprout, Holly and Scrooge.'

The tiny puppies opened their eyes and began to crawl, and soon they took their first steps. They started to grow to look their mum. Their coats were growing and they were all playing and having lots of fun together.

'Don't worry Jack, it won't be long until all of my puppies find new homes, leaving us to play together, like old times!'

'That's good, Lilly! They really do wear me out, but I'm sure I will miss them all very much too.'

Lilly and her six puppies played around the kitchen, weaving in and out of the dining table and chairs, and through the whole house. Oh how they played and played, until they felt very tired and fell asleep together.

One day, in early February, the garden had turned white due to the heavy snowfall. The puppies have never seen or felt soft snow on their little wet noses before.

The backdoor opened. Lilly, Scrooge, Holly, Noel, Cracker, Sprout and Humbug, all ran outside into the freshly fallen white snow. Jack followed and joined in the games with Lilly and the puppies.

'This is such fun, Jack! Look at my puppies - they love it! Oh, it's wonderful. This is snow!'

They all ran around and around. Holly was rolling on her back, playing with her mum, and having so much fun!

A robin perched on a garden trowel close to Sprout. It chirped and chirped surprising Sprout, who had never seen a bird before.

Sprout gazed for a while and suddenly barked, sending the little red robin flying away.

As excited families arrived and chose their special little puppy, Lilly watched on sadly, realising that she did not want them to leave.

Jack looked sad too, but he pretended to be happy that the puppies were leaving. The puppies themselves were happy with their new families, cuddling and playing, and then came the time to say farewell. One by one each puppy said goodbye to Lilly and Jack, excited to see their new homes.

'Are you OK, Lilly? Come here, let's have a cuddle. You still have me, you know? I'm not going anywhere. I love you very much.'

'Oh, Jack! I love you, too! I have you, and you have me. We will always have each other. Of course I will miss my beautiful puppies, but the time is right for them to leave and go to their new homes.'

The house seemed very quiet and empty after Lilly's six puppies had left, leaving Jack and Lilly alone.

After a long walk through the muddy woods, Lilly cheered up, running through the wet grass and diving into her favourite pool.

Lilly was so wet and muddy, and so very smelly. She was back to her old self again.